Fruit of the Spirit

for

PreK–1st Grade

100 Sight Words

Written and Illustrated by:
Adrienne Vance

Fruit of the Spirit
for
PreK–1ˢᵗ Grade
100 Sight Words

Copyright © 2024 All rights reserved by Adrienne Vance

Advance Editing and Publishing LLC

All rights reserved. No part of this book may be used or reproduced by any means, graphic, electronic, or mechanical, including photocopying, recording, taping, or by any information storage retrieval system, without the written permission of the publisher except in the case of brief quotations adequately cited and embodied in critical articles.

Editing by: Advance Editing and Publishing LLC

Printed in the United States of America

~Dedication~

I dedicate this book to my fruitful children:

Jaden, Daniel, Isaiah, and Israel.

Preface

Fruit of the Spirit for Children is a collection of twelve children's books. They are interactive with coloring pages and journal entries for fun and encouraging ways for children to grow and express their faith in God according to Galatians 5:22-23, *"The Fruit of the Spirit is love, joy, peace, patience, kindness, goodness, faithfulness, gentleness, and self-control."*

In addition to the Fruit of the Spirit book series, "Fruit of the Spirit for Middle Schoolers" is written for preteens and middle school-aged youth. "Fruitful I AM Affirmations", "A Fruitful Devotional", and "A Fruitful Bible Study" are written for adults. "Fruitful I AM Affirmations for Teens" and "Fruit of the Spirit: Devotional Journal for Teens" are written for high schoolers and those entering adulthood. This book series is for the entire family!

Given that God reveals His name to Moses as "Yahweh", which means "I AM WHO I AM" (*Exodus 3:14*), this fruitful series is purposed to inspire readers to seek the Great I AM's affirmations of love as our ultimate source for identity, validation, and guidance. Jesus, whose name is Yeshua in Hebrew and who is God manifested within humanity, proclaimed to the world that He is the True Vine (*John 15*), who by our faith in Him and through the power of His Holy Spirit, we grow to be more fruitful in His Kingdom as children of God.

One of Yahweh's first commands to humanity, which is the creation that was created in His image, was to be fruitful (*Genesis 1:26-28*). Yeshua as the True Vine, who compared His blood of salvation to grape wine (*Luke 22:20*), taught us that the greatest commands from Yahweh are to love Him with all our hearts, minds, and souls and to love people as we love ourselves (*Matthew 22:37-39*). Grapes are one fruit with each grape in a cluster as an expression of that fruit. Likewise, all the Fruit of the Spirit are expressions of Yahweh's love, which is why the word "fruit" is singular.

The revelation is that the first command to humanity to be fruitful was a command to love. The Creator's expectation of His creation to be His image on the earth has not changed. God is the same yesterday, today, and forever. God is love (*1John 4:16*), and as His creation, we are commanded to love. This book series about the Fruit of the Spirit is for people of all ages and is written in obedience to God to help edify the body of Christ (*Ephesians 4:11-13*), by encouraging the Church to be obedient to the Sovereign King's first command to humanity, "Be Fruitful!"

During my personal worship time with God, He revealed to me that just like the rainbow is hidden in pure white light until it is seen through a prism, so are the varying expressions of God's love expressed with more distinction through the Holy Spirit living within us. Also, grapes are one fruit with many expressions, like the rainbow light of love. God showed me a vision in my prayer time and told me to write a book series about what I saw. In the vision, God merged a rainbow with a cluster of grapes to teach me about the existence of rainbow grapes. As I researched what God showed me in the vision, I learned that in nature, grapes experience the veraison stage in which they are referred to as "rainbow grapes" because of their multicolored expressions before reaching maturity.

As children of Yahweh, we express all the colors of the rainbow light of God's pure love as we mature our faith in Christ Jesus. Love is a rainbow in which we can taste the many flavors of each colorful light like rainbow grapes on the True Vine. Every time we eat the fruit of Yahweh's love through reading His Word, worshipping in prayer, and loving people, the more our eyes are opened to see the world through eyes of love as Jesus does. The more fruit of the Spirit we eat, the more fruitful we become. We are what we eat. This Fruit of the Spirit book series is for your entire family! Taste and see how sweet God's fruit of love is!

~Prayer of Salvation~

Heavenly Father, I ask for your forgiveness of my wrongs. I believe you are Jesus Christ, who died on the cross for my sins, raised yourself back to life in three days, and sent back your Holy Spirit to help me be who you created me to be. I ask your Holy Spirit to live within me. I give you all my mind, heart, soul, body, and life to you! Help me be fruitful in your Kingdom! Thank you for loving, forgiving, and saving me in Christ Jesus' name! Amen!

*It is highly recommended that a more fluent reader helps the child to read the words that are unfamiliar, especially the highlighted sight words. As the child becomes more acclimated to the sight words, the fluent reader should gradually allow the child to identify the sight words independently. Repetition is the key to learning. Therefore, this book is meant to be read multiple times until the child has mastered all the words in this book, preferably learning the sight words first. As the more fluent reader, I immensely encourage you to practice exemplifying the fruit of patience and kindness as you lovingly help the little reader to acquire reading skills that will bear fruit for the rest of their lives.

Have fun coloring with crayons or colored pencils on the coloring pages. Please, do not use markers, which may leak through the pages. For the journal entries, feel free to express your thoughts!

God is the Great I AM WHO I AM!

God named Himself,

"I AM WHO I AM."

God told Moses to call Him, "I AM".

God is the Great

I AM WHO I AM!

I AM is everything we need.

God is the Great

I AM WHO I AM!

Joy, Peace, Patience, Kindness,

Goodness, Faith

God is the Great

I AM WHO I AM!

Gentleness, Responsibility

God is the Great

I AM WHO I AM!

Jesus is I AM's first fruit of love.

Because of Jesus, I am fruitful!

God is the Great

I AM WHO I AM!

I am a Child of God!

God chose me to be His child.

I do good things to make God smile.

I am always on God's heart and mind.

God made me special,

so I am one of a kind.

God came down from heaven

to become a child.

His name was Jesus Christ.

He was meek and mild.

As a man, He taught people

how to be fruitful and pray.

Jesus Christ showed everybody how to

love and live God's way.

He gave His life on a cross,

so I can be free to be me.

Three days later, He came back to life.

In Him, I believe.

He gave me His Holy Spirit. Now, He

smiles and nods,

Because I am fruitful like Him.

I am a child of God!

I am Loved!

I am loved whether

I'm here or there.

God is love, and

He is everywhere.

When I awake and

say morning prayer,

God's smile shines on me

with loving care.

All throughout the day,

God leads the way.

Because I love Him,

I will obey.

As I sleep, He keeps me

safe from harm.

I am covered with love in God's arms.

Jesus' love is as pure as a dove.

I'm fruitful, because

I'm purely loved.

His fruit of love is more than enough.

I love everyone, because

I am loved!

I am Joyful!

God loves everyone,

each girl and boy.

Knowing I am loved

fills me with joy!

When I'm feeling sad, alone, and down,

I remind myself

I'm heaven bound.

One day I'll have

my mansion and crown.

That thought turns all

my frowns upside down!

I know that God is

always around.

I smile knowing

I am safe and sound.

Each child of God

is His daughter or son.

I share my smiles

with everyone.

I am joyful, because

I am loved.

He showers His

blessings from above.

I am Peaceful.

When things confuse me,

God gives me peace.

When I am fearful,

God gives me peace.

When people are mean,

God gives me peace.

When things aren't easy,

God gives me peace.

When I want to quit,

God gives me peace.

When I lose my friends,

God gives me peace.

When family die and rest in peace,

Knowing we'll meet again

gives me peace.

Because Jesus is

the Prince of Peace,

I share with the world

His fruit of peace.

You can be peaceful,

just taste and see!

When you trust in God,

His peace is sweet!

I am Patient.

Sometimes I rush and

don't want to wait.

I wonder what is

taking all day

Do I really have to

wait so long?

If I hurry things,

would I be wrong?

The Bible tells me

to wait on God.

God is my shepherd, my staff, and rod.

He teaches me

the right way to go,

when to agree, and

when to say, "No."

Jesus is always

patient with me.

So, I will wait for Him

patiently.

Sometimes blessings

test our patience.

When I trust His love,

I am patient.

I am Kind.

Sometimes kind people

are hard to find.

That is why I

made up in my mind

To share kindness with everyone.

In their clouds, my light

shines like the Son

My kind deeds are

the actions of love

Through me, they see

God's heart from above.

God created me

one of a kind.

In God's family,

I am His kind.

My kindness is

how I resemble

The Lord's character

as His temple.

The kindness of Jesus

proves His love.

My kindness proves

I'm sent from above.

Be Kind

I am Good!

I am trying my best

to be good.

I try to do the things

that I should.

I do not always

get it all right.

I am not flawless,

and that's alright.

When I fall short

as I am striving,

I get back up and keep on trying.

Jesus sees in my

heart, mind, and soul

I trust Him to help me

reach my goals.

God thinks I'm perfect

just as I am.

He covers sins with

blood of the lamb.

Jesus gave me

the best life He could,

my new life in Christ.

Now, I am good!

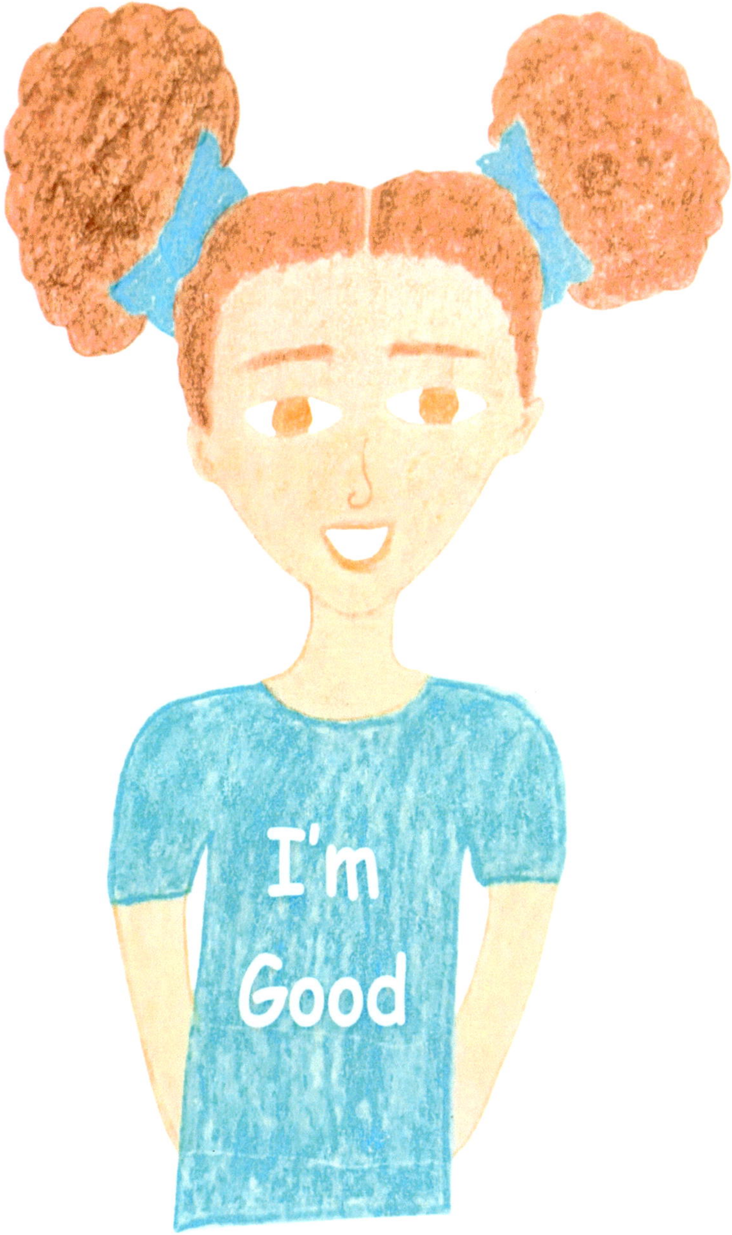
I'm
Good

I am Faithful!

I believe everything God says.

He is faithful

when I am faithless.

He believes in me

when I do not.

He helps me see

my story with His plot.

When I lack faith,

God's Word strengthens me.

God's Bible stories

encourage me.

When I have done

all the things I can,

Jesus sees my faith

and understands.

He loves my faith

even when it's small.

God helps my faith

grow up big and tall.

I believe God

can do anything!

That is why I serve Him

as my King!

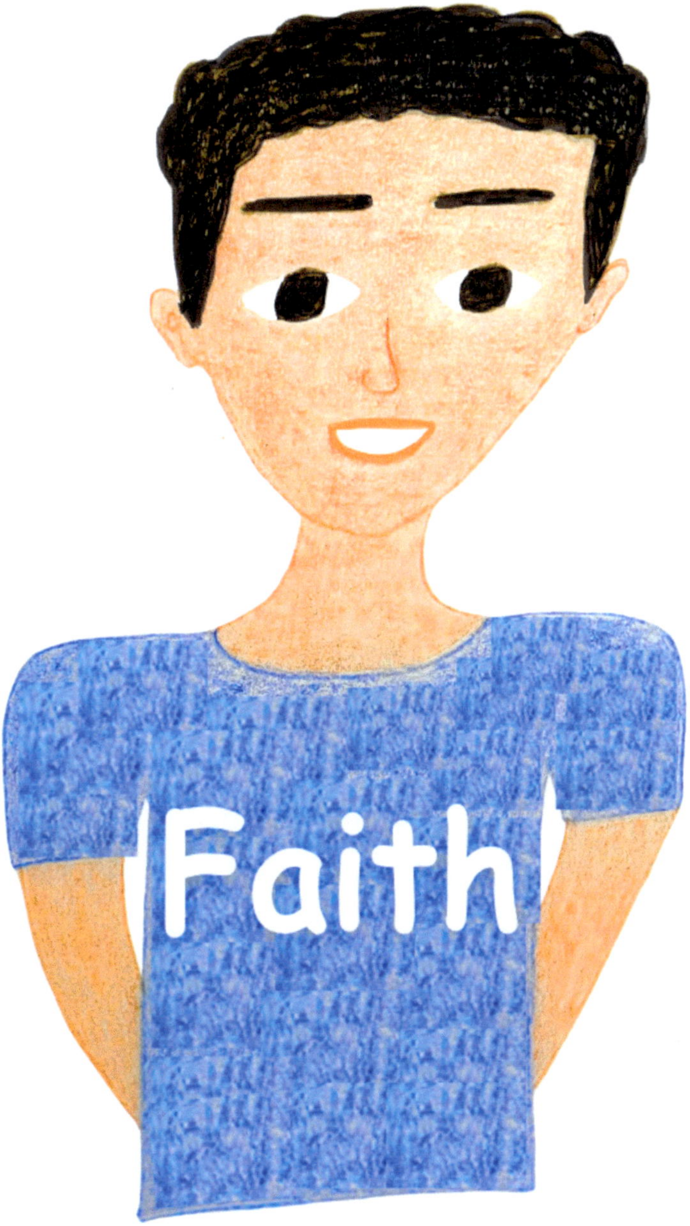
Faith

I am Gentle.

Gently God wakes me
in the morning.
On me His blessings
He is pouring.
Like dew in the morning rests gently
On petals and leaves,
He rests on me
to grace my day
with His gentle love,
He showers His
blessings from above.
Tough love is okay,
but not every day.

The tender love of God
shows the way
to live like Jesus,
humble and wise.
He understands
my laughter and cries.
His strength is
His gentle love for us.
His gentleness
is more than enough!

Gentle Lady

I am Responsible.

Occasionally, I'm forgetful.

I'm trying to be

responsible.

When I check my list,

I remember.

I'm trying to be

responsible.

From time to time,

I procrastinate.

I'm trying to be

responsible.

When I time my plans,

I reach my goals.

I'm trying to be

responsible.

I do not always

pay attention.

I am trying to have

self-control.

I pray that Jesus

helps me to listen.

With God's help, I am responsible!

I'm Responsible

My God is in Control!

There is only one God. There is no other god but Yahweh. There are not many gods or two or any number but one. Many people think that because God had done so many amazing things then there may be more than one god. Their way of looking at the world and trying to find out about how everything came into life is not always right.

This is why God had His people to write parts in the Bible about how He would use His words to make all things come into being. Its words teach us about how God made outer space and the earth. From long ago, we were a part of God's plan from the beginning when this world was first covered with water. What God said had to come to pass. So, God used words to make the world. No one could ever do this but God. Out of nothing would come something every time God said anything.

It was with God's words that land and living creatures were called out of the water. When we look at all that God did, we should think about how powerful He is. God had Moses to write ten rules that each one of God's people had to obey and told him that Yahweh was God's name, which says, I AM WHO I AM, meaning God can do any impossible thing.

God's son, Jesus, taught that there are two rules which are the most important. These rules teach us to love only one God, Yahweh, and to love other people. God came to the world as a baby at a time when people did many bad things. He grew up and taught people good lessons to live by and did many miracles.

Then, after teaching them these good ways like this book is teaching you, Jesus did something else that was His most amazing miracle of all. He brought Himself back to life after bad people killed Him on a cross, which proved that He is God. They were bad but Jesus was and is good.

Now, by believing in Jesus and living a fruitful life of love, we will share God's love with everyone. God loves you so much that He knows the number of all the hairs on your head and cares about every part of your life. God loves each girl and boy in the whole world even if she or he are not perfect and does not know all the stories in his or her Bible.

The Bible is written to help them learn how to become the best girl or boy that she or he can be. Its teachings are good and helps us to be fruitful with love, joy, peace, kindness, goodness, faithfulness, gentleness, self-control and patience. God has a special plan for his and her life and always has love for them.

God's love will never run out. People can never use up God's love. God may not be happy about our mistakes, but He is an amazingly loving God. Even if there were millions of people needing God's love at one time, God's love would be more than enough. We love an all-powerful God who will never go away and leave us alone. God is always by your side and will be with you at home or anywhere you go.

I am Fruitful!

I am loved!

I am joyful!

I am peaceful.

I am patient.

I am kind.

I am good!

I am faithful!

I am gentle.

I am responsible!

I am fruitful!

LOVE never ends . . .

~About the Author~

The illustrator and author, Adrienne Vance, is a child of God, the Great I AM, through her faith in Christ Jesus. She is blessed to be the loving mother of her four amazing sons: Jaden, Daniel, Isaiah, and Israel. She is a native of Madison County, Mississippi. She earned her Bachelor of Arts in Christian Studies and Philosophy with a concentration in Philosophy and a minor in Biology from Mississippi College, a Christian University. She is pursuing her Master of Arts in Teaching at Belhaven University, a Leader in Christian Worldview Education. Adrienne Vance has served as an educator teaching English Language Arts and Writing for eight years.

She was licensed and ordained as a minister of the Gospel of Jesus Christ in 2010 by the late great Pastor A. D. McGruder at St. Paul Missionary Baptist Church in Canton, MS. She has been an in-person member for three years and continues to serve as an e-member of The Potter's House led by her pastor, Bishop T.D. Jakes, where she has grown under his ministry for over twenty years. She is the CEO of Advance Editing & Publishing LLC, a business that edits and publishes Christian books. She is also the host of the House of Faith with Adrienne Vance where she leads Biblical teachings and interviews featured guests from various spheres of influence. She is graced to be a mother, minister, educator, entrepreneur, talk show host, and author.

Reference

The World English Bible is a 1997 revision of the American Standard Version of the Holy Bible, first published in 1901. It is in the Public Domain.

Special Thank You!

I greatly appreciate you investing time of your life into reading this work from God's heart through my heart to your heart! I encourage you to share this book with others to help advance the Great I AM's Kingdom on Earth through the fruit of the Spirit! I love you dearly! More importantly, Jesus Christ, the one true living God, loves you infinitely!

Contact Information

Follow the author on social media @ Adrienne Vance on Facebook and Instagram.
Subscribe to my YouTube channel entitled,
"House of Faith with Adrienne Vance".
To book speaking engagements with Adrienne Vance, email: info@houseoffaithministries.com
Request Advance Editing & Publishing LLC to edit your Christian book: www.houseoffaithministries.com
You can purchase more books by Adrienne Vance on Amazon, Barnes and Noble, and Books-a-Million.
I immensely appreciate your loving support!

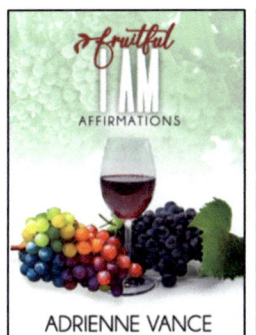

Fruitful I AM Affirmations
ADRIENNE VANCE

a Fruitful Devotional
40 DAYS OF I AM AFFIRMATIONS
ADRIENNE VANCE

A Fruitful Bible Study
Fruit of the Spirit in Galatians 5:22-23
ADRIENNE VANCE

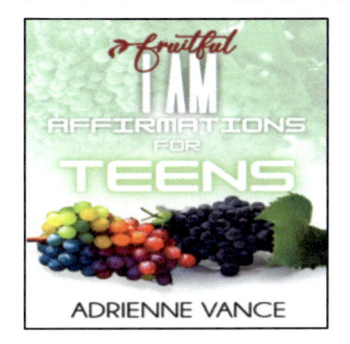

Fruitful I AM Affirmations for TEENS
ADRIENNE VANCE

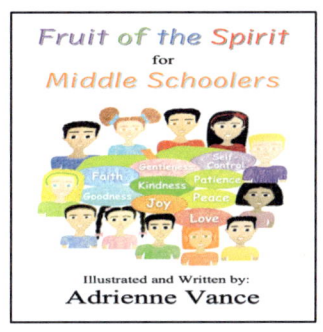

Fruit of the Spirit for Middle Schoolers
Illustrated and Written by: Adrienne Vance

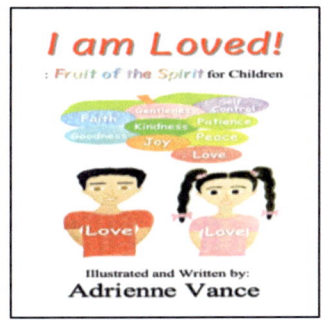

I am Loved!
: Fruit of the Spirit for Children
Illustrated and Written by: Adrienne Vance

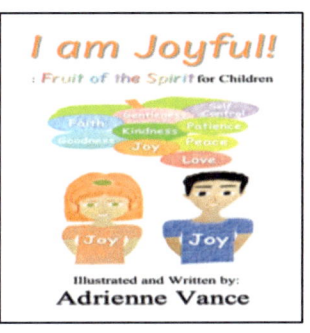

I am Joyful!
: Fruit of the Spirit for Children
Illustrated and Written by: Adrienne Vance

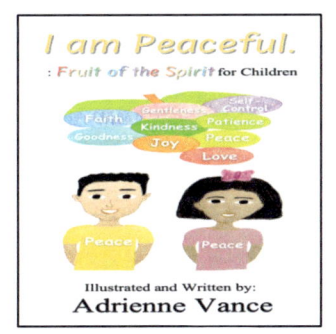

I am Peaceful.
: Fruit of the Spirit for Children
Illustrated and Written by: Adrienne Vance

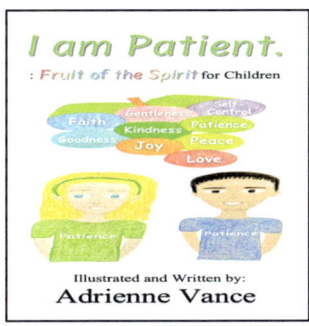

I am Patient.
: Fruit of the Spirit for Children
Illustrated and Written by: Adrienne Vance

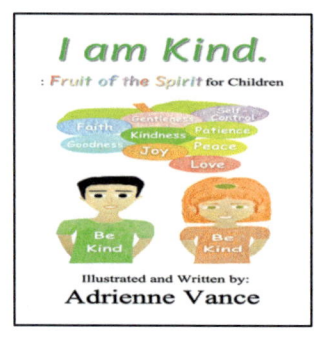

I am Kind.
: *Fruit of the Spirit* for Children

Illustrated and Written by:
Adrienne Vance

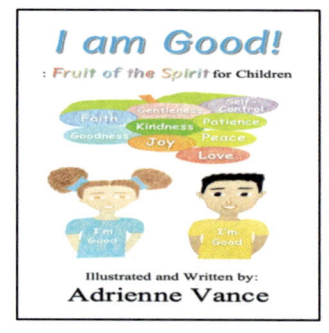

I am Good!
: *Fruit of the Spirit* for Children

Illustrated and Written by:
Adrienne Vance

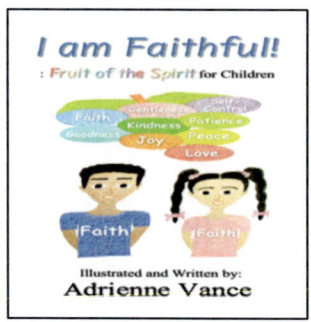

I am Faithful!
: *Fruit of the Spirit* for Children

Illustrated and Written by:
Adrienne Vance

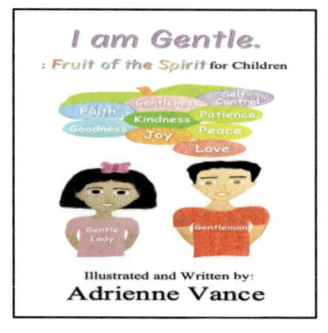

I am Gentle.
: *Fruit of the Spirit* for Children

Illustrated and Written by:
Adrienne Vance

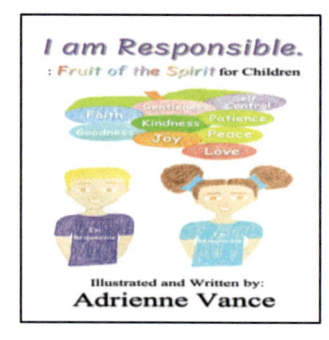

I am Responsible.
: *Fruit of the Spirit* for Children

Illustrated and Written by:
Adrienne Vance

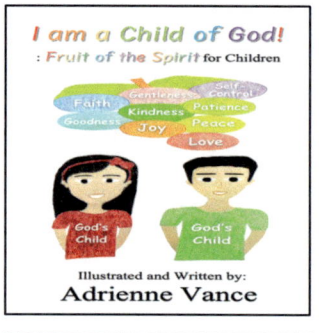

I am a Child of God!
: *Fruit of the Spirit* for Children

Illustrated and Written by:
Adrienne Vance

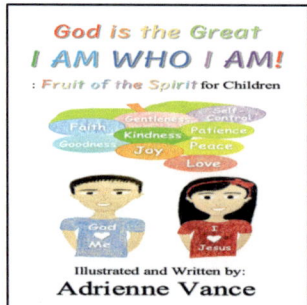

God is the Great
I AM WHO I AM!
: *Fruit of the Spirit* for Children

Illustrated and Written by:
Adrienne Vance

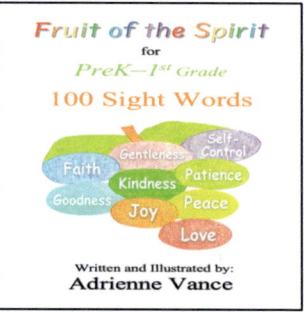

Fruit of the Spirit
for
PreK—1st Grade
100 Sight Words

Written and Illustrated by:
Adrienne Vance

Thank you!

~Adrienne Vance

Made in the USA
Columbia, SC
12 September 2024